Girl Dinner

Publications International, Ltd.

Typeface of book title, chapter titles and step numbers copyright © Shutterstock.com.

Photograph on front cover and page 159 copyright © Shutterstock.com.

Pictured on the front cover: Basic Board (page 158).

Pictured on the back cover (clockwise from top left): Caprese Sandwiches (page 85), Peppermint Chip Cake in a Cup (page 172), Fabulous Feta Frittata (page 147), Avocado Toast (page 96) and Choco-Peanut Butter Popcorn Chow (page 149) and Fiesta Corn Salad (page 36).

ISBN: 978-1-63938-609-3

Manufactured in China.

8 7 6 5 4 3 2 1

Let's get social!
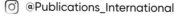 @Publications_International
@PublicationsInternational
www.pilbooks.com

Contents

Dips for Dinner

Jalapeño Feta Dip

makes about 1 cup dip

1 jalapeño pepper, halved, stemmed and seeded

½ red onion, halved and separated

3 tablespoons plus 1 teaspoon olive oil, divided

8 ounces feta cheese

1 tablespoon water

Toasted baguette slices, pita bread wedges and/or cut-up vegetables

1 Preheat oven to 400°F. Place jalapeño and onion on small baking sheet; drizzle with 1 teaspoon oil and stir to coat. Arrange vegetables cut sides down on baking sheet. Bake 20 minutes or until vegetables are softened and slightly charred around edges. Let stand until cool enough to handle.

2 Scrape skin from jalapeño with paring knife. Coarsely chop jalapeño and onion.

3 Combine cheese, remaining 3 tablespoons oil and water in food processor; process until smooth and fluffy. Add vegetables; pulse 6 to 8 times or until blended but still chunky. Serve with toast and/or vegetables. Store in airtight container in the refrigerator up to 1 week.

Everything Bagel Dip
makes 2 cups dip

2 large bagels, cut vertically into thin (¼-inch) slices

1 container (12 ounces) whipped cream cheese

1½ tablespoons green onion, finely chopped (green part only)

4 teaspoons everything bagel seasoning

1 Preheat oven to 350°F. Spread bagel slices on baking sheet; spray generously with nonstick cooking spray. Bake 7 to 8 minutes or until golden brown, stirring once.

2 Meanwhile, combine cream cheese, green onion and bagel seasoning in medium bowl; mix well. Serve with bagel chips.

Note If you don't have everything bagel seasoning, substitute 1 teaspoon dried minced onion, 1 teaspoon granulated garlic, 1 teaspoon sesame seeds, 1 teaspoon poppy seeds and ¼ teaspoon kosher salt.

Italian-ish Cheese Spread

makes about 2 cups spread

1 cup ricotta cheese

6 ounces cream cheese, softened

1 medium onion, chopped

2 tablespoons grated Parmesan cheese

1 tablespoon capers, drained and rinsed

2 anchovy fillets, mashed *or* 2 teaspoons anchovy paste

1 teaspoon dry mustard

1 teaspoon paprika

½ teaspoon hot pepper sauce

Cut-up vegetables, crackers or toasted French bread slices

1 Beat ricotta cheese and cream cheese in large bowl with electric mixer at medium speed 3 minutes or until well blended. Stir in onion, Parmesan cheese, capers, anchovies, mustard, paprika and hot pepper sauce; mix well. Serve immediately or cover and refrigerate 1 day to allow flavors to blend.

2 Serve dip with vegetables and/or toast. Store in airtight container in refrigerator up to 1 week.

Tip For a party, serve the dip in a hollowed-out cabbage or bell pepper. Leftover spread makes a great pizza topping or sandwich spread.

Apricot and Brie Dip

makes 3 cups dip

½ cup dried apricots, finely chopped

⅓ cup plus 1 tablespoon apricot preserves, divided

¼ cup apple juice

1 round (2 pounds) Brie cheese, rind removed and cut into cubes

Assorted crackers

Slow Cooker Directions

1 Combine dried apricots, ⅓ cup apricot preserves and apple juice in small or medium slow cooker. Cover; cook on HIGH 40 minutes.

2 Stir in cheese. Cover; cook on HIGH 30 minutes or until melted. Stir in remaining 1 tablespoon preserves. Serve with crackers.

Note For a quick snack, microwave individual portions of leftovers until heated through. Leftover dip also makes an excellent sandwich spread.

Quick Homemade Hummus

makes about 2 cups hummus

1 can (about 15 ounces) chickpeas, rinsed and drained

½ cup tahini

2 tablespoons cold water

2 tablespoons lemon juice

½ teaspoon salt

½ teaspoon cumin

½ teaspoon curry powder

¼ cup packed fresh parsley

Pita chips and cut-up vegetables

1 Place chickpeas, tahini, water, lemon juice, salt, cumin and curry powder in food processor; process 1 to 2 minutes or until smooth and fluffy. Add parsley; process until blended.

2 Serve with pita chips and/or vegetables.

Tip Use leftover hummus to make a Mediterranean Vegetable Sandwich (page 58) or Mediterranean Salad (page 48).

Cherry-Cheese Spread

makes about 2 cups spread

1 package (8 ounces) cream cheese, softened

¼ cup half-and-half or whipping cream

1 tablespoon sugar

1 tablespoon cherry-flavored liqueur*

1 cup fresh sweet cherries, pitted and chopped

¼ cup sliced almonds, toasted

Toasted plain or cinnamon-raisin bagels or bagel chips

If desired, omit cherry liqueur and substitute 1 tablespoon milk plus 1 teaspoon additional sugar.

1 Place cream cheese, half-and-half, sugar and liqueur in medium bowl of electric mixer; beat at low speed until just blended. Increase to high speed; beat until smooth. Gently fold in fresh cherries. (Do not overmix or spread will turn purple.)

2 Place spread in bowl; sprinkle with sliced almonds. Serve with toasted bagels or plain crackers.

Tip To quickly soften cream cheese, unwrap cream cheese and place on a plate. Microwave on HIGH for 20 to 30 seconds to soften.

Tzatziki Cucumber Dip

makes 3 cups dip

1 cup peeled diced
  English cucumber

2 cups plain Greek
  yogurt

Grated peel of 1 lemon

3 tablespoons fresh
  lemon juice

2½ tablespoons minced
  fresh mint

2 tablespoons olive oil

1 tablespoon minced
  garlic

2 teaspoons salt

1½ teaspoons white wine
  vinegar

Carrot sticks, grape
  tomatoes, trimmed
  green onions,
  zucchini sticks and/or
  bell pepper strips

1 Wrap cucumber in clean dish towel or paper towels. Twist towel over sink to squeeze juice from cucumber.

2 Combine cucumber, yogurt, lemon peel, lemon juice, mint, oil, garlic, salt and vinegar in medium bowl; mix well. Serve immediately or cover and refrigerate 2 hours. Serve with vegetables.

Cheesy Artichoke Dip

makes 2 cups dip

8 garlic-and-herb spreadable cheese wedges

1 can (about 14 ounces) artichokes, rinsed, drained and coarsely chopped

½ cup (2 ounces) shredded mozzarella cheese

¼ cup shredded Parmesan cheese

1 tablespoon sour cream, plus additional if necessary

2 teaspoons fresh lemon juice

¼ teaspoon ground red pepper

Cut-up vegetables and/or pretzel chips crackers

1 Mash cheese wedges in medium microwavable bowl until smooth. Add artichokes, mozzarella cheese, Parmesan cheese, 1 tablespoon sour cream, lemon juice and red pepper. Add additional sour cream, if necessary, to thin dip to desired consistency. Microwave on HIGH 1 minute; stir. Microwave at 30-second intervals until heated through, stirring after each interval.

2 Serve warm with vegetables and/or pretzel chips.

Cheesy Fondue

makes about 4 cups

2 cups (8 ounces) shredded Swiss cheese

2 cups (8 ounces) shredded Monterey Jack cheese

2 tablespoons all-purpose flour

1½ cups dry white wine or apple juice

Dash ground nutmeg

Dash ground red pepper

Cubed French bread

Granny Smith apple slices

1 Combine Swiss cheese, Monterey Jack cheese and flour in large bowl; toss to coat.

2 Bring wine to a simmer in fondue pot or medium heavy saucepan over medium heat. Gradually add cheese mixture by handfuls until melted, stirring constantly. Stir in nutmeg and pepper.

3 Keep warm over low heat, stirring occasionally. Serve with bread and apples for dipping.

Tip Use leftover fondue as part of grilled cheese sandwich filling.

Tirokafteri
(Spicy Greek Feta Spread)

makes 2 cups spread

2 small hot red peppers
½ small clove garlic
1 block (8 ounces) feta
   cheese
¾ cup plain Greek yogurt
1 tablespoon lemon juice
½ teaspoon salt
   Toasted sliced French
   bread and/or cut-up
   fresh vegetables

1 Preheat oven to 400°F. Place peppers on small piece of foil on baking sheet. Bake 15 minutes or until peppers are soft and charred. Cool completely. Scrape off skin with paring knife. Cut off top and remove seeds. Place peppers in food processor. Add garlic; pulse until finely chopped.

2 Add cheese, yogurt, lemon juice and salt; pulse until well blended but still chunky. Serve with bread or vegetables. Store leftovers in airtight container in refrigerator 1 week.

Pretzel Dippers

makes 48 dippers and ⅔ cup dip

⅓ cup spicy brown mustard

3 tablespoons whipped butter or softened butter

2 tablespoons mayonnaise

1 package frozen soft pretzels (6 pretzels)

24 thin slices salami, cut into halves

10 ounces Swiss cheese, cut into scant ½-inch cubes

1 Whisk mustard, butter and mayonnaise in small bowl until well blended.

2 Dampen pretzels with water and sprinkle with salt from package. Microwave 2 minutes or until pretzels are warm.

3 Cut each pretzel into 8 pieces. Wrap half slice of salami around each pretzel piece; top with cheese cube and secure with toothpick. Serve with mustard sauce for dipping.

Cheesecake Dip

makes ¾ cup dip

½ cup sour cream
2 ounces cream cheese, softened
3 tablespoons whipping cream or milk
2 tablespoons sugar
½ teaspoon vanilla
Ground nutmeg
Bananas for dipping

1 Place sour cream, cream cheese, cream, sugar and vanilla in blender; blend until smooth.

2 Place dip in serving bowl; sprinkle with nutmeg. Serve with bananas for dipping.

Variation Substitute coconut extract for the vanilla to make a tropical inspired dipping sauce.

Quick Cheese Log

makes about 2 cups spread

1 container (8 ounces) whipped chive cream cheese

1 cup (4 ounces) shredded Cheddar cheese

⅓ cup chopped walnuts

Crackers, potato chips and/or cut-up vegetables

1 Combine cream cheese and Cheddar cheese in medium bowl; mix well. Shape into log about 5 inches long.

2 Spread nuts on piece of plastic wrap or waxed paper. Place log on nuts and carefully roll to coat with nuts. Place on serving plate; serve immediately with crackers or wrap in plastic wrap and refrigerate up to 1 day.

27

Picante Vegetable Dip

makes about 1⅔ cups dip

⅔ cup sour cream
½ cup picante sauce
⅓ cup mayonnaise
¼ cup finely chopped green or red bell pepper
2 tablespoons finely chopped green onion
¾ teaspoon garlic salt
Cut-up vegetables and/or tortilla chips

1 Combine sour cream, picante sauce, mayonnaise, bell pepper, green onion and garlic salt in medium bowl until well blended.

2 Serve immediately with vegetables and/or chips or cover and refrigerate several hours to allow flavors to blend.

Dill Cheese Spread

makes about ½ cup spread

¼ cup cream cheese with herbs and garlic

2 tablespoons mayonnaise

2 tablespoons sour cream

2 teaspoons chopped fresh dill

¼ teaspoon salt

Garlic-flavored melba toast rounds

1 Combine cream cheese, mayonnaise, sour cream, dill and salt, if desired, in small bowl.

2 Serve immediately with melba toast or cover and refrigerate 1 hour for flavors to blend.

Warm Salsa and Goat Cheese Dip

makes about 1½ cups

1¼ cups medium salsa
1 log (4 ounces) goat cheese (not crumbles)
2 tablespoons coarsely chopped fresh cilantro
Tortilla chips or sliced French bread

1 Preheat oven to 350°F.

2 Pour salsa into 9-inch pie plate or 2-quart baking dish. Cut goat cheese crosswise into 5 pieces; place on salsa.

3 Bake about 20 minutes or until salsa is bubbly and cheese is heated through. Sprinkle with cilantro. Serve warm with tortilla chips.

Peanutty Banana Dip

makes about 1 cup dip

½ cup sliced banana

⅓ cup creamy peanut butter

2 tablespoons milk

1 tablespoon honey

½ teaspoon vanilla

⅛ teaspoon ground cinnamon

Sliced apples and/or celery sticks

1 Combine banana, peanut butter, milk, honey, vanilla and cinnamon in blender; blend until smooth.

2 Serve with apples or celery for dipping.

Spinach, Artichoke and Feta Dip

makes about 1½ cups

½ cup frozen chopped spinach, thawed and squeezed dry

1 cup (4 ounces) crumbled feta cheese

½ teaspoon black pepper

1 cup marinated artichokes, undrained

Pita chips and/or cut-up vegetables

1 Place spinach in small microwavable bowl; microwave on HIGH 2 minutes.

2 Place cheese and pepper in food processor. Pulse until finely chopped. Add artichokes and spinach; process 30 seconds until well blended but still chunky (do not purée). Serve with pita chips and/or vegetables.

Garlic and Herb Dip

makes about 1¼ cups

1 cup sour cream
¼ cup mayonnaise
2 tablespoons chopped green onion
1 teaspoon dried basil
½ teaspoon dried tarragon
1 clove garlic, minced
¼ teaspoon salt
¼ teaspoon black pepper
Pita chips and/or cut-up vegetables

1 Whisk sour cream, mayonnaise, green onion, basil, tarragon, garlic, salt and pepper in medium bowl. Serve immediately or refrigerate 2 hours to allow flavors to blend.

2 Serve with pita chips and/or vegetables.

Snacky Salads

Turkey Caesar Salad

makes 2 to 4 servings

10 ounces sliced oven-roasted deli turkey

1 head romaine lettuce, torn into pieces

¾ cup Caesar dressing

1 cup croutons

¼ cup shredded Parmesan cheese

Black pepper

1 Cut turkey into strips.

2 Combine lettuce and dressing in large bowl; toss to coat. Top with turkey, croutons, cheese and black pepper.

Fiesta Corn Salad

makes 4 to 6 servings

1 cup plain yogurt

3 tablespoons minced onion

1½ tablespoons lime juice

1 clove garlic, minced

1 teaspoon ground cumin

1 teaspoon chili powder

¼ teaspoon salt

4 cups frozen corn, cooked according to package directions

1½ cups shredded red cabbage

1 large tomato, chopped

1 green bell pepper, finely chopped

5 slices bacon, cooked and crumbled (optional)

1 cup coarsely crushed tortilla chips

1 cup (4 ounces) shredded Cheddar cheese

1 Whisk yogurt, onion, lime juice, garlic, cumin, chili powder and salt in large bowl. Add corn, cabbage, tomato and bell pepper; mix lightly. Stir in bacon, if desired.

2 Serve immediately or refrigerate several hours for flavors to blend. Sprinkle with chips and cheese just before serving.

Greek Salad

makes 6 servings

Salad

3 medium tomatoes, cut into 8 wedges each

1 green bell pepper, cut into 1-inch pieces

½ English cucumber (8 to 10 inches), quartered lengthwise and sliced crosswise

½ red onion, thinly sliced

½ cup pitted Kalamata olives

1 block (8 ounces) feta cheese, cut into ½-inch cubes

Dressing

6 tablespoons extra virgin olive oil

3 tablespoons red wine vinegar

1 to 2 cloves garlic, minced

¾ teaspoon dried oregano

¾ teaspoon salt

¼ teaspoon black pepper

1 For salad, combine tomatoes, bell pepper, cucumber, onion and olives in large bowl. Top with cheese.

2 For dressing, whisk oil, vinegar, garlic, oregano, salt and black pepper in small bowl until well blended. Pour over salad; stir gently to coat.

Tortellini with Artichokes, Olives and Feta Cheese

makes 2 to 4 servings

1 package (9 ounces) refrigerated cheese-filled spinach tortellini

1 jar (4 ounces) marinated artichoke heart quarters, drained*

¼ cup sliced pitted black or kalamata olives

1 carrot, diagonally sliced

¼ cup crumbled feta cheese

¼ cup cheese-garlic Italian salad dressing

Black pepper

*For additional flavor, add some artichoke marinade to tortellini with salad dressing.

1 Cook pasta according to package directions. Drain and rinse under cold water until cool.

2 Combine pasta, artichokes, olives, carrot and cheese in large bowl. Add salad dressing; toss to coat. Season to taste with pepper.

Texas Caviar

makes about 9 cups

1 tablespoon vegetable oil

1 cup fresh corn (from 2 to 3 ears) or thawed frozen corn

2 cans (about 15 ounces each) black-eyed peas, rinsed and drained

1 can (about 15 ounces) black beans, rinsed and drained

1 cup halved grape tomatoes

1 bell pepper (red, orange, yellow or green), finely chopped

½ cup finely chopped red onion

1 jalapeño pepper, seeded and minced

2 green onions, minced

¼ cup chopped fresh cilantro

2 tablespoons red wine vinegar

1 tablespoon lime juice

1 teaspoon salt

1 teaspoon sugar

½ teaspoon ground cumin

½ teaspoon dried oregano

2 cloves garlic, minced

¼ cup olive oil

1 Heat vegetable oil in large skillet over high heat. Add corn; cook and stir about 3 minutes or until corn is beginning to brown in spots. Place in large bowl. Add beans, tomatoes, bell pepper, onion, jalapeño, green onions and cilantro.

2 Combine vinegar, lime juice, salt, sugar, cumin, oregano and garlic in small bowl. Whisk in olive oil in thin, steady stream until well blended. Pour over vegetables; stir to coat.

3 Serve immediately or refrigerate 2 hours or overnight for flavors to blend; stir in additional lime juice and additional salt, if desired, just before serving.

Note Serve Texas Caviar as a dip for a crowd with corn chips or tortilla chips. It also makes a great packable lunch or side dish.

Rigatoni Salad

makes about 8 servings

12 ounces uncooked rigatoni pasta

1 package (8 ounces) fresh snow peas or sugar snap peas

1 to 2 cups chopped greens, such as arugula, frisée or any crisp lettuce

8 ounces cherry tomatoes, halved

1 red or yellow bell pepper, thinly sliced

½ red onion, thinly sliced

⅓ cup sliced black olives

⅓ to ½ cup Italian salad dressing

Grated Parmesan cheese (optional)

1 Cook pasta in large saucepan of boiling salted water according to package directions for al dente, adding peas during last 1 minute of cooking. Drain and rinse under cold water until cool. Place in large bowl.

2 Add greens, tomatoes, bell pepper, onion and olives. Top with dressing; toss gently. Sprinkle with cheese, if desired.

Italian Crouton Salad

makes 6 servings

6 ounces French or Italian bread

¼ cup plain yogurt

¼ cup red wine vinegar

2 tablespoons olive oil

1 tablespoon water

3 cloves garlic, minced

½ teaspoon salt

¼ teaspoon black pepper

6 medium plum tomatoes, sliced (about 3¾ to 4 cups)

½ medium red onion, thinly sliced

3 tablespoons sliced fresh basil

2 tablespoons finely chopped fresh parsley

1 bag (about 5 ounces) Italian salad mix (optional)

2 tablespoons grated Parmesan cheese

1 Preheat broiler. Cut bread into ¾-inch cubes. Place in single layer on baking sheet. Broil 4 inches from heat 3 minutes or until bread is golden, stirring every 30 seconds to 1 minute. Place croutons in large bowl.

2 Whisk yogurt, vinegar, oil, water, garlic, salt and pepper in large bowl until blended. Add tomatoes, onion, basil, parsley and croutons; toss to coat.

3 Cover and refrigerate 30 minutes or up to 1 day. (Croutons will be softer the following day.) Serve salad over lettuce, if desired. Sprinkle with cheese.

Tip If you don't want to bother with the broiler, cut the bread into slices that will fit in your toaster and toast until golden brown. Cool and cut into cubes.

Mediterranean Salad

makes 4 servings

2 cups chopped iceberg lettuce

2 cups baby spinach

2 cups diced cucumbers

1 cup diced cooked chicken

1 cup chopped roasted red peppers

1 cup grape tomatoes, halved

1 cup quartered artichoke hearts

¾ cup crumbled feta cheese

½ cup chopped red onion

1 cup hummus

½ teaspoon Italian seasoning

1 Divide lettuce and spinach among four salad bowls or plates; top with cucumbers, chicken, roasted peppers, tomatoes, artichokes, cheese and onion.

2 Top salad with hummus; sprinkle with Italian seasoning.

Garlic Bread and Salmon Salad

makes 4 cups salad

2 slices day-old whole wheat bread

1 clove garlic, cut in half

1 can (about 6 ounces) salmon, drained and flaked

½ cup chopped green onions

1 cup cherry or grape tomatoes, halved

1 tablespoon olive oil

2 tablespoons white wine vinegar

1 tablespoon tomato juice

¼ teaspoon salt

¼ teaspoon black pepper

2 tablespoons minced fresh basil

1 Toast bread in toaster until golden brown. Rub one side of each bread slice with garlic; discard garlic. Cut bread into 1-inch pieces.

2 Combine salmon, green onions and tomatoes in large serving bowl.

3 Whisk oil, vinegar, tomato juice, salt and pepper in small bowl. Pour over salmon mixture. Add garlic bread cubes and toss again. Sprinkle with basil.

Mediterranean Pasta Salad

makes 2 to 4 servings

2 ounces uncooked bow tie pasta

1 cup canned chickpeas, rinsed and drained

1 cup cooked canned artichoke hearts, rinsed, drained and quartered

¾ cup halved zucchini slices

¼ cup chopped red onion

3 tablespoons lemon juice

2 tablespoons olive oil

½ teaspoon Italian seasoning

¼ teaspoon salt

⅛ teaspoon black pepper

⅛ teaspoon garlic powder

2 tablespoons crumbled feta cheese

1 Cook pasta in large saucepan of salted boiling water according to package directions for al dente. Drain and run under cold water until cool. Place in large bowl; add chickpeas, artichoke hearts, zucchini and onion.

2 Whisk lemon juice, oil, Italian seasoning, salt, pepper and garlic powder in small bowl until well blended. Drizzle over pasta mixture; toss to coat. Top with cheese before serving.

Random Sandwiches

Cranberry Turkey Sandwiches

makes 4 sandwiches

- ¼ cup cream cheese
- ¼ cup cranberry sauce or chutney
- 2 tablespoons chopped toasted* walnuts
- 8 slices multigrain or whole wheat bread, lightly toasted
- ½ pound sliced deli smoked turkey breast
- 1 cup packed mesclun or spring salad mixed greens *or* 4 red leaf lettuce leaves

To toast walnuts, cook in medium skillet over medium heat 3 to 4 minutes or until lightly browned and fragrant, stirring occasionally.

1 Combine cream cheese and cranberry sauce in small bowl; mix well. Stir in walnuts.

2 Spread mixture on toast slices. Layer turkey and greens on four slices; top with remaining four slices. Cut diagonally in half.

Quick Waffled Quesadilla

makes 1 quesadilla

2 (6-inch) flour tortillas

½ cup (2 ounces) shredded Cheddar cheese or Monterey Jack cheese

¼ cup finely chopped poblano pepper or jalapeño pepper

1 small plum tomato, chopped

⅛ teaspoon ground cumin

Salt and black pepper

½ ripe medium avocado, chopped

1 to 2 tablespoons chopped fresh cilantro

Juice of ½ lime

1 Preheat classic waffle maker to medium. Coat both sides of each tortilla with nonstick cooking spray.

2 Top one tortilla with cheese, poblano pepper, tomato and cumin. Season with salt and pepper. Top with other tortilla. Place on waffle maker; close, pressing down slightly. Cook 3 minutes or until golden brown and cheese is melted.

3 Carefully remove tortilla. Cut into quarters. Top with avocado, cilantro and lime juice.

Tip Squeeze lime juice from remaining half of lime over remaining avocado; cover and store in refrigerator for another use.

Mediterranean Vegetable Sandwich

makes 4 sandwiches

½ cup plain hummus

½ jalapeño pepper, seeded and minced

¼ cup minced fresh cilantro

8 slices whole wheat bread

4 leaves lettuce (leaf or Bibb lettuce)

2 tomatoes, thinly sliced

½ cucumber, thinly sliced

½ red onion, thinly sliced

½ cup thinly sliced peppadew peppers or sweet Italian peppers

4 tablespoons (1 ounce) crumbled feta cheese

1 Combine hummus, jalapeño and cilantro in small bowl; mix well.

2 Spread about 1 tablespoon hummus mixture on one side of each bread slice. Layer half of bread slices with lettuce, tomatoes, cucumber, onion, peppadew peppers and cheese; top with remaining bread slices.

Tuna Melt

makes 8 open-faced sandwiches

¾ cup mayonnaise

2 teaspoons lemon juice

1 teaspoon salt

⅛ teaspoon black pepper

1 can (12 ounces) solid white albacore tuna, drained

1 can (12 ounces) chunk light tuna, drained

1 stalk celery, finely chopped (about ½ cup)

¼ cup minced red onion

8 slices bread

8 slices Cheddar or American cheese

2 tablespoons butter

Optional toppings: tomato slices, onion slices, pickles and/or avocado

1 Combine mayonnaise, lemon juice, salt and pepper in large bowl. Add tuna, celery and red onion; mix well.

2 Divide tuna among bread slices; top each with cheese. Heat 1 tablespoon butter in large skillet over medium heat until melted. Add half of sandwiches; cover and cook until bread is toasted and cheese is melted. Repeat with remaining ingredients, or reserve for future dinners. Serve with desired toppings.

Tip If you don't want to bother with a sandwich, tuna salad can be a dinner on its own served with crackers, pretzel chips, potato chips or cucumber slices.

Bavarian Pretzel Sandwiches

makes 4 sandwiches

4 frozen soft pretzels, thawed

1 tablespoon German mustard or whole grain brown mustard

2 teaspoons mayonnaise

8 slices Black Forest ham

4 slices Gouda cheese

1 tablespoon water

1 Preheat oven to 350°F. Line baking sheet with parchment paper.

2 Carefully slice each pretzel in half crosswise using serrated knife. Combine mustard and mayonnaise in small bowl. Spread mustard mixture on bottom halves of pretzels. Top with two ham slices, one slice cheese and top halves of pretzels.

3 Place sandwiches on prepared baking sheet. Brush tops of sandwiches with water; sprinkle with salt from packet. Bake 8 minutes or until cheese is melted.

Note For cold sandwiches, bake the pretzels according to package directions. When they are cool enough to handle, slice them and top with the sandwich fillings.

Grilled Prosciutto, Brie and Fig Sandwiches

makes 2 sandwiches

¼ cup fig preserves

4 slices (½ to ¾ inch thick) Italian or country bread

Black pepper

4 to 6 ounces Brie cheese, cut into ¼-inch-thick slices

2 slices prosciutto (about half of 3-ounce package)

¼ cup baby arugula

1½ tablespoons butter

1 Spread preserves over two bread slices. Sprinkle pepper generously over preserves. Top with cheese, prosciutto, arugula and remaining bread slices.

2 Heat medium cast iron skillet over medium heat 5 minutes. Add 1 tablespoon butter; swirl to melt and coat bottom of skillet. Add sandwiches; cook over medium-low heat about 5 minutes or until bottoms of sandwiches are golden brown.

3 Turn sandwiches and add remaining ½ tablespoon butter to skillet. Tilt pan to melt butter and move sandwiches so butter flows underneath. Cover with lid or foil; cook about 5 minutes or until cheese is melted and bread is golden brown.

Spanakopita Sandwiches

makes 4 sandwiches

1 tablespoon butter

¼ cup finely chopped onion

1 clove garlic, minced

1 package (10 ounces) frozen chopped spinach, thawed and squeezed dry

4 ounces crumbled feta cheese

¼ teaspoon dried oregano

Pinch of ground nutmeg

Black pepper

4 medium croissants

8 slices (1 ounce each) Monterey Jack cheese

1 Melt butter in large skillet over medium heat. Add onion and garlic; cook and stir 5 minutes or until onion is tender. Add spinach; cook 5 minutes or until spinach is dry. Remove from heat; stir in feta cheese, oregano and nutmeg. Season to taste with black pepper.

2 Divide spinach mixture evenly among croissant bottoms; top with Monterey Jack cheese and croissant tops.

3 Wipe out skillet with paper towel; heat over medium heat. Add sandwiches; cover with lid or foil. Cook sandwiches over low heat 5 to 6 minutes or until cheese melts and bottoms of sandwiches are golden brown.

Vegetable-Bean Quesadillas

makes 8 quesadillas

1 tablespoon canola oil

1 cup sliced onion

1 can (about 15 ounces) black beans, rinsed and drained

1 cup sliced green bell pepper

1 cup sliced red bell pepper

½ teaspoon ground cumin

¼ teaspoon ground red pepper

8 (8-inch) whole grain tortillas

1 cup (4 ounces) shredded Cheddar cheese

Salsa and sour cream (optional)

1 Heat oil in large nonstick skillet over medium-high heat. Add onion; cook and stir 2 minutes or until translucent. Add beans, bell peppers, cumin and red pepper; cook and stir 3 minutes or until bell peppers are crisp-tender.

2 Heat medium nonstick skillet over medium heat. Place one tortilla in skillet. Spread about ⅓ cup vegetables on half of tortilla; sprinkle with 2 tablespoons cheese. Fold tortilla over filling and cook until light brown on bottom. Turn and brown other side. Repeat with remaining ingredients. Cut into wedges. Serve with salsa and sour cream, if desired.

Tip If you have leftover Texas Caviar (page 42), you can use it instead of the filling.

Egg Salad Sandwiches

makes 4 open-faced sandwiches

6 eggs

3 tablespoons mayonnaise

½ cup finely chopped green onions

1½ tablespoons sweet or dill pickle relish

¼ to ½ teaspoon celery seed

¼ teaspoon salt

⅛ teaspoon black pepper

4 slices whole grain bread

2 cups packed spring greens

1 Bring large saucepan of water to a boil. Carefully add eggs using slotted spoon. Cook 11 minutes. Drain and run under cold water or let stand in ice water until cool.

2 Peel eggs and place eggs in medium bowl; mash with fork to desired consistency. Stir in mayonnaise, green onions, pickle relish, celery seed, salt and pepper; mix well.

3 Serve egg salad on bread with greens.

Tip Serve leftover egg salad as a quick meal with kettle chips for scooping.

Stuffed Focaccia Sandwich

makes 4 sandwiches

- 1 container (about 5 ounces) soft cheese with garlic and herbs
- 1 (10-inch) round herb or onion focaccia, cut in half horizontally
- ½ cup thinly sliced red onion
- ½ cup coarsely chopped pimiento-stuffed green olives, drained
- ¼ cup sliced mild banana peppers
- 4 ounces thinly sliced deli hard salami
- 6 ounces thinly sliced oven-roasted turkey breast
- 1 package (⅔ ounce) fresh basil, stems removed

1 Spread soft cheese over cut sides of focaccia. Layer bottom half evenly with remaining ingredients. Cover sandwich with top half of focaccia; press down firmly.

2 Cut sandwich into four pieces. Serve immediately or wrap individually in plastic wrap and refrigerate until ready to serve.

Chicken Fajita Sandwich

makes 4 sandwiches

2 tablespoons olive oil, plus additional for brushing sandwiches

1 small onion, sliced

1 red bell pepper, sliced

12 ounces chicken tenders, cut in half lengthwise and crosswise

1 cup guacamole

4 slices (1 ounce each) pepper jack cheese

2 packages (10 ounces each) 8-inch mini pizza crusts (8 total)

1 Heat 2 tablespoons oil in large nonstick skillet over medium-high heat. Add onion and bell pepper; cook and stir 5 minutes or until crisp-tender. Remove vegetables with slotted spoon to bowl. Add chicken to skillet; cook and stir 4 minutes or until chicken is cooked through. Remove from skillet; wipe out skillet with paper towel.

2 Layer guacamole, chicken, vegetables and cheese evenly on four pizza crusts; top with remaining four pizza crusts. Brush sandwiches lightly with additional oil.

3 Heat same skillet over medium heat. Cook sandwiches in batches 4 to 5 minutes per side or until cheese melts and sandwiches are golden brown. Cut into wedges to serve.

Tip Cold leftovers are like a bonus zero-effort extra meal, but you can also easily reheat them if you want. Reheat sandwich wedges in a skillet over medium heat until hot, turning once.

Chickpea Salad

makes 2 cups salad

- 1 can (about 15 ounces) chickpeas, rinsed and drained
- 1 stalk celery, chopped
- 1 dill pickle, chopped (about ½ cup)
- ¼ cup finely chopped red or yellow onion
- ⅓ cup mayonnaise
- 1 teaspoon lemon juice
- ¼ teaspoon salt
- Black pepper
- Whole grain bread, toasted
- Lettuce and tomato slices

1 Place chickpeas in medium bowl. Coarsely mash with potato masher, leaving some beans whole.

2 Add celery, pickle and onion; stir to blend. Add mayonnaise and lemon juice; mix well. Taste and add ¼ teaspoon salt or more, if desired. Sprinkle with pepper, if desired; mix well.

3 Serve on toast with lettuce and tomato, if desired.

Tip Leftover salad is great with rice or grains. Heat a pouch of precooked brown rice or mixed grains and make a bowl out of it with some chickpea salad, and any leftover veggies you have on hand.

Chicken Pesto Flatbreads

makes 2 sandwiches

2 (6- to 7-inch) round flatbreads or Greek-style pita bread rounds (no pocket)

2 tablespoons prepared pesto

1 cup grilled chicken strips

4 slices (1 ounce each) mozzarella cheese

1 plum tomato, cut into ¼-inch slices

3 tablespoons shredded Parmesan cheese

1 Place flatbreads on work surface. Spread 1 tablespoon pesto over half of each flatbread. Place chicken on opposite half of bread; top with mozzarella cheese, tomato and Parmesan cheese. Fold pesto-topped bread half over filling.

2 Spray grill pan or nonstick skillet with nonstick cooking spray or brush with vegetable oil; heat over medium-high heat. Cook sandwiches 3 minutes per side or until bread is toasted, cheese begins to melt and sandwiches are heated through.

Buffalo Chicken Wraps

makes 4 wraps

1 package (12 ounces) grilled chicken breast strips

¼ cup buffalo wing sauce

2 cups broccoli slaw mix

2 tablespoons blue cheese salad dressing

4 (8-inch) whole wheat tortillas, warmed

1 Heat chicken according to package directions. Place in medium bowl; stir in buffalo wing sauce.

2 Combine broccoli slaw and blue cheese dressing in another medium bowl; mix well.

3 Layer chicken and broccoli slaw over center of third of each tortilla. Roll up to enclose filling. Cut in half diagonally.

Grilled Banana and Chocolate Panini

makes 6 sandwiches

¼ cup (½ stick) butter, softened

1 frozen pound cake (about 10 ounces), thawed and cut into 12 (½-inch-thick) slices

1 cup chocolate-hazelnut spread

3 ripe bananas, cut lengthwise into slices

Ground cinnamon

1 Spread butter over one side of each pound cake slice.

2 For each panini, lay one slice pound cake, buttered side down, on work surface. Spread chocolate-hazelnut spread over cake slice; top with banana slices and sprinkle with cinnamon. Top with second cake slice, buttered side up.

3 Spray indoor grill or panini press with nonstick cooking spray; heat to medium. Cook sandwiches 2 minutes or until cake is golden brown.

Peanutty Carrot Roll-Ups

makes 2 roll-ups

½ cup peanut butter

2 (6- to 7-inch) whole wheat or spinach tortillas

½ cup finely chopped apple

¼ cup shredded carrot

2 tablespoons honey

1 Spread peanut butter evenly over one side of each tortilla.

2 Sprinkle apple and carrot over peanut butter to cover three fourths of the tortilla.

3 Drizzle honey evenly over apple and carrot. Starting from the edge nearest filling, roll up tortillas. Cut tortillas in half crosswise. Serve immediately or wrap tightly in plastic wrap and refrigerate until ready to eat.

Toasted Peanut Butter Sandwiches

makes 4 sandwiches

⅔ cup peanut butter

2 tablespoons toasted wheat germ

1 tablespoon honey

8 slices firm whole wheat or multigrain bread

1 ripe banana, sliced

2 eggs

⅓ cup orange juice

1 tablespoon grated orange peel

1 tablespoon butter

1 Combine peanut butter, wheat germ and honey in small bowl. Spread evenly on one side of each bread slice. Place banana slices on top of peanut butter mixture on four slices of bread. Top with remaining bread slices, peanut butter side down. Lightly press together.

2 Whisk eggs, orange juice and orange peel in shallow dish. Dip sandwiches in egg mixture, coating both sides.

3 Melt butter in large nonstick skillet over medium heat. Add sandwiches; cook until golden brown, turning once.

Turkey, Havarti and Apple Roll-Ups

makes 4 roll-ups

4 slices (1 ounce each) Havarti cheese

4 slices (1 ounce each) turkey

6 tablespoons Dijon-style mayonnaise

1 medium apple, cut into slices or sticks

1 Place one slice of cheese on each slice of turkey and spread with mayonnaise.

2 Top with apple slices and roll up.

Bacon and Egg Croissants

makes 4 sandwiches

1 teaspoon vinegar*

4 eggs

2 croissants, halved and toasted

4 slices tomato

½ avocado, sliced crosswise

8 slices bacon, crisp-cooked

Mayonnaise

Chopped chives and/or alfalfa sprouts

Adding vinegar to the water helps keep the egg white intact while poaching.

1 Fill wide deep skillet with about 1½ inches water; add vinegar. Bring to a simmer. Break one egg into shallow cup or saucer; gently slide egg into saucepan. Repeat with remaining eggs.

2 Cook eggs 3 to 4 minutes or until set. Carefully remove eggs with slotted spoon; drain on paper towels.

3 Place croissant half on each plate. Layer tomato, avocado and bacon on croissants. Top with eggs, mayonnaise, chives and/or sprouts.

Caprese Sandwiches

makes 4 sandwiches

8 ounces fresh mozzarella cheese, cut into slices

8 slices multigrain or whole wheat bread, toasted

8 slices ripe tomato

2 teaspoons olive oil

Salt and black pepper

¼ cup sliced or chopped fresh basil

1 Place one cheese slice on each of four slices of toast. Toast in toaster oven or heat in microwave on HIGH 20 to 30 seconds to soften cheese.

2 Top each sandwich with two tomato slices; drizzle with oil. Season with salt and pepper; sprinkle with basil. Top with remaining toast; cut in half diagonally.

Totally Toasts

Pear-Topped Grahams

makes 4 toasts

¼ cup cream cheese,
   softened

4 whole cinnamon
   graham crackers

4 teaspoons raspberry
   fruit spread

1 pear, halved, cored
   and cut into 16 slices

1 Spread 1 tablespoon cream cheese evenly over each cracker. Spread 1 teaspoon fruit spread over cream cheese.

2 Arrange four pear slices overlapping slightly on top of each cracker. Serve immediately.

Toasted Pesto Crostini
makes 12 toasts

¼ cup thinly sliced fresh basil or chopped fresh dill

¼ cup grated Parmesan cheese

3 tablespoons mayonnaise

1 clove garlic, minced

12 French bread slices, about ¼ inch thick

1 tablespoon plus 1 teaspoon chopped fresh tomato

1 green onion, sliced

1 Preheat broiler.

2 Combine basil, cheese, mayonnaise and garlic in small bowl; mix well.

3 Arrange bread slices in single layer on ungreased baking sheet or broiler pan. Broil 6 to 8 inches from heat 30 to 45 seconds or until bread is lightly toasted. Turn bread slices over; spread evenly with basil mixture. Broil 1 minute or until lightly browned. Top evenly with tomato and green onion; serve immediately.

Garden Bruschetta

makes 2 toasts

1 medium zucchini, cut into ¼-inch-thick diagonal slices

1 large shallot or small red onion, thinly sliced

1 tablespoon olive oil
Salt and black pepper

2 slices artisan whole wheat bread

1 clove garlic, crushed

2 small plum tomatoes, thinly sliced

¼ teaspoon dried oregano

1 tablespoon chopped fresh basil (optional)

3 jumbo pimiento-stuffed olives, thinly sliced

3 tablespoons shredded Parmesan cheese, divided

1 Preheat oven to 425°F. Spray large baking sheet with nonstick cooking spray. Arrange zucchini and shallot on baking sheet; drizzle with oil and season with salt and pepper. Roast 15 minutes or until tender.

2 Rub bread slices with garlic; discard garlic. Place bread on another baking sheet; bake 5 to 7 minutes or until bread is toasted.

3 Layer tomatoes on bread; season with salt and pepper and sprinkle with oregano and basil, if desired. Top with zucchini, shallot, olives and cheese.

4 Preheat broiler. Broil toasts 20 seconds or until cheese is melted and browned.

Chickpea, Roasted Pepper and Olive Toasts

makes 24 toasts

½ cup drained pitted black olives

½ cup drained pimiento-stuffed green olives

2 cloves garlic, peeled

1 can (about 15 ounces) chickpeas, rinsed and drained

1 cup chopped drained roasted red peppers

¼ cup olive oil

Salt and black pepper

24 (½-inch) toasted French bread slices

1 Place black and green olives in food processor. Pulse until olives are coarsely chopped. Transfer to small bowl.

2 With food processor running, drop garlic through feed tube. Add chickpeas and roasted peppers; process until almost smooth. Add oil; process until smooth. Transfer to medium bowl; season with salt and black pepper.

3 Spread 2 tablespoons chickpea mixture on each bread slice; top with 1 tablespoon olive mixture. Serve at room temperature.

Classic Tomato Bruschetta

makes 2 cups topping

1 tablespoon olive oil

1 small clove garlic, minced

2 cups chopped seeded tomatoes (3 medium)

1/8 teaspoon salt

Black pepper

Toasted Italian bread slices

Slivered fresh basil

1 Heat oil and garlic in small skillet over medium heat 2 minutes, stirring occasionally. Remove from heat. Stir in tomatoes, salt and pepper; mix well.

2 Serve tomato mixture on toasts; top with basil.

Tip Use leftover bruschetta mixture as a pizza or pasta topping.

Avocado Toast

makes 4 toasts

½ cup thawed frozen peas

2 teaspoons lemon juice

1 teaspoon minced fresh tarragon

¼ teaspoon plus ⅛ teaspoon salt, divided

⅛ teaspoon black pepper

1 teaspoon olive oil

1 tablespoon pepitas (raw pumpkin seeds)

4 slices hearty whole grain bread, toasted

1 avocado

1 Combine peas, lemon juice, tarragon, ¼ teaspoon salt and pepper in small food processor; pulse until blended but still chunky. (Or combine all ingredients in small bowl and mash to desired consistency with fork.)

2 Heat oil in small saucepan over medium heat. Add pepitas; cook and stir 1 to 2 minutes or until toasted. Transfer to small bowl; stir in remaining ⅛ teaspoon salt.

3 Spread about 1 tablespoon pea mixture over each slice of bread.

4 Cut avocado in half lengthwise around pit; remove pit. Thinly slice avocado in the shell; use a spoon to scoop slices out of the shell. Arrange avocado slices on toasts; top with toasted pepitas.

Spanish Ham and Cheese Toasts

makes 24 toasts

1 package (4 ounces) goat cheese, at room temperature

1 teaspoon ground cumin

½ teaspoon smoked paprika or paprika

24 (½-inch) toasted French bread slices

½ cup chopped fresh parsley

8 slices Serrano ham or proscuitto, cut crosswise into thirds

1 Place goat cheese in small bowl. Add cumin and paprika; stir until well blended and uniform in color. Cover and let stand 30 minutes.

2 Spread goat cheese mixture on bread slices; sprinkle with parsley. Top each toast with one piece of ham. Serve at room temperature.

Ham and Cheese Snacks

makes 4 servings

- 8 thin slices ham (about 6 ounces total)
- 2 tablespoons honey mustard
- 8 thin slices Muenster cheese (about 4 ounces total)
- Thin pretzel crisps or crackers

1 Spread each ham slice with about ¾ teaspoon mustard. Top one slice of ham with one slice of cheese; top with second slice of ham and cheese to create two double ham and cheese stacks.

2 Starting with long side, roll up each ham and cheese stack into spiral. Wrap tightly in plastic wrap; refrigerate 30 minutes or up to 24 hours.

3 Cut each ham and cheese roll into ½-inch slices. Serve on pretzel crisps.

Pizza-Type Stuff

Pepperoni Pizza Bagels

makes 8 pizzas

4 plain or sesame seed bagels

½ cup marinara or pizza sauce

1 cup (4 ounces) shredded mozzarella cheese

¼ cup mini pepperoni slices

Dried oregano

1 Preheat oven to 400°F. Line baking sheet with parchment paper or foil.

2 Cut bagels in half crosswise. Spread 1 tablespoon marinara sauce over each cut half; top with cheese and pepperoni. Place on prepared baking sheet.

3 Bake 8 to 10 minutes or until cheese is melted and beginning to brown. Sprinkle with oregano.

Quattro Formaggio Pizza

makes 1 pizza

½ cup pizza or marinara sauce

1 (12-inch) prepared pizza crust

4 ounces shredded or thinly sliced provolone cheese

2 ounces Asiago or brick cheese, thinly sliced

1 cup (4 ounces) shredded smoked or regular mozzarella cheese

¼ cup grated Parmesan or Romano cheese

1 Preheat oven to 450°F.

2 Spread pizza sauce evenly over pizza crust; place on baking sheet. Sprinkle with provolone and Asiago cheeses; top with mozzarella and Parmesan cheeses.

3 Bake 14 minutes or until crust is golden brown and cheeses are melted. Cut into wedges.

Tortilla Pizza Wedges

makes 4 pizzas

1 tablespoon vegetable oil

1 cup frozen corn, thawed

1 cup thinly sliced mushrooms

4 (6-inch) corn tortillas

¼ cup marinara or pizza sauce

1 tablespoon chopped jalapeño pepper

¼ teaspoon dried oregano

¼ teaspoon dried marjoram

½ cup (2 ounces) shredded mozzarella cheese

1 Preheat oven to 450°F. Heat oil in large skillet over medium heat. Add corn and mushrooms; cook and stir 5 minutes or until mushrooms are tender.

2 Place tortillas on baking sheet. Bake 4 minutes or until edges begin to brown.

3 Combine marinara sauce, jalapeño, oregano and marjoram in small bowl. Spread evenly over tortillas. Top with corn and mushrooms; sprinkle with cheese.

4 Bake 4 to 5 minutes or until cheese is melted and pizzas are heated through. Cut into wedges.

Fig, Bacon and Blue Cheese Pizza

makes 1 pizza

1 (12-inch) prepared pizza crust

2 tablespoons olive oil, divided

1 red onion, thinly sliced

½ cup (2 ounces) shredded Monterey Jack cheese

3 tablespoons fig jam

4 slices turkey bacon or regular bacon

⅓ cup sliced dried figs

½ cup crumbled gorgonzola cheese

2 tablespoons balsamic glaze

Baby arugula (optional)

1 Preheat oven to 450°F. Place pizza crust on baking sheet or pizza pan. Brush with 1 tablespoon oil.

2 Heat remaining 1 tablespoon oil in large skillet over medium heat. Add onion; cook and stir 10 minutes or until soft and lightly browned. Spread over pizza crust; sprinkle with Monterey Jack cheese. Dot with jam and top with bacon and figs. Sprinkle with gorgonzola cheese.

3 Bake about 10 minutes or until crust is lightly browned and cheese is melted. Drizzle balsamic glaze over pizza and top with arugula, if desired. Cut into wedges.

Pizza Sandwich

makes 4 to 6 sandwich wedges

1 loaf (12 ounces)
  focaccia
½ cup pizza sauce
20 slices pepperoni
8 slices (1 ounce each)
  mozzarella cheese
1 can (2¼ ounces) sliced
  mushrooms, drained
  Red pepper flakes
  (optional)
  Olive oil

1 Cut focaccia horizontally in half. Spread cut sides of both halves with pizza sauce. Layer bottom half with pepperoni, cheese and mushrooms; sprinkle with red pepper flakes, if desired. Cover with top half of focaccia. Brush top and bottom of sandwich with oil.

2 Heat large nonstick skillet over medium heat. Add sandwich; press down with spatula or weigh down with small plate. Cook sandwich 4 to 5 minutes per side or until cheese is melted and sandwich is golden brown. Cut into wedges to serve.

Note Focaccia can be found in the bakery section of most supermarkets. It is often available in different flavors, such as tomato, herb, cheese or onion.

Caprese Pizza

makes 6 servings

1 loaf (16 ounces) frozen pizza dough or bread dough, thawed

1 container (12 ounces) bruschetta sauce (see Note)

1 container (8 ounces) pearl-size fresh mozzarella cheese (perlini), drained*

Chopped fresh basil (optional)

*If pearl-size mozzarella is not available, use one (8-ounce) ball of fresh mozzarella and chop into ¼-inch pieces.

1 Preheat oven to 400°F. Spray large baking sheet with nonstick cooking spray.

2 Roll out dough on lightly floured surface into 15×10-inch rectangle. Place on prepared baking sheet. Cover loosely with plastic wrap; let rest 10 minutes. Meanwhile, place bruschetta sauce in colander; let drain 10 minutes.

3 Prick surface of dough several times with fork. Bake 10 minutes. Spread drained bruschetta sauce over crust; top with cheese.

4 Bake 10 minutes or until cheese is melted and crust is golden brown. Serve warm; garnish with basil.

Note Bruschetta sauce is a mixture of diced fresh tomatoes, garlic, basil and olive oil. It is typically found in the refrigerated section of the supermarket with other prepared dips such as hummus. You can also use leftover topping from Classic Tomato Bruschetta (page 94).

Pepperoni Bread

makes about 6 servings

1 package (about 14 ounces) refrigerated pizza dough

8 slices provolone cheese

20 to 30 slices pepperoni (about half of 6-ounce package)

½ teaspoon Italian seasoning

¾ cup (3 ounces) shredded mozzarella cheese

½ cup grated Parmesan cheese

1 egg, beaten

Marinara sauce, heated

1 Preheat oven to 400°F. Unroll dough on sheet of parchment paper with long side in front of you.

2 Arrange half of provolone slices over bottom half of dough, cutting to fit as necessary. Top with pepperoni; sprinkle with ¼ teaspoon Italian seasoning. Top with mozzarella cheese, Parmesan cheese and remaining provolone slices; sprinkle with remaining ¼ teaspoon Italian seasoning.

3 Fold top half of dough over filling; press edges with fork or pinch edges to seal. Slide bread on parchment onto baking sheets. Brush with egg.

4 Bake 16 minutes or until crust is golden brown. Slide bread on parchment onto wire rack; cool slightly. Cut crosswise into slices; serve with marinara sauce.

Down Under Pizza

makes 1 pizza

1 (12- to 14-inch) prepared pizza crust

1 tablespoon olive oil

1 cup (4 ounces) shredded Monterey Jack cheese or mozzarella cheese

6 ounces cooked shrimp

1 can (8 ounces) pineapple chunks, drained

½ green bell pepper, diced

3 tablespoons shredded Parmesan cheese

¼ cup chopped fresh cilantro

Red pepper flakes

1 Preheat oven to 450°F.

2 Place prepared crust on pizza pan. Brush crust with olive oil and sprinkle with Monterey Jack cheese. Top with shrimp, pineapple, bell pepper and Parmesan cheese.

3 Bake about 8 minutes or until crust is deep golden and cheese is melted. Sprinkle with cilantro and red pepper. Cut into wedges.

Note In Australia, this pizza topping combination is one of the most popular.

Green Garden Pizza

makes 4 to 6 servings

2 packages (8 ounces each) refrigerated crescent roll dough

12 ounces cream cheese, softened

1 cup sour cream

2 tablespoons dry ranch salad dressing mix (about ½ package)

¾ cup cucumber slices, cut in half

2 cups broccoli florets

½ cup carrot slices

¾ cup grape tomatoes, cut in half

1 Preheat oven to 375°F. Place dough in single layer in ungreased 15×10-inch baking sheet. Press onto bottom and up sides of baking sheet, sealing perforations. Bake 13 to 17 minutes or until brown. Cool completely.

2 Beat cream cheese in large bowl with electric mixer at medium speed until fluffy. Add sour cream and salad dressing mix; beat until blended. Spread over cooled crust.

3 Arrange rows of cucumber slices, broccoli florets, carrot slices and tomato halves on pizza. Cut pizza into 24 rectangles. Serve immediately or cover and refrigerate for up to 1 day.

Flatbread with Ricotta, Peaches and Arugula

makes 2 flatbreads

- ½ cup baby arugula
- 1 teaspoon olive oil
- ½ teaspoon lemon juice
- ½ cup ricotta cheese
- 2 tablespoons finely chopped fresh basil
- ½ teaspoon salt
- ⅛ teaspoon black pepper
- 2 naan breads
- 1 peach, thinly sliced
- 2 teaspoons balsamic vinegar or balsamic glaze
- Flaky sea salt

1 Preheat oven to 400°F. Line baking sheet with parchment paper. Combine arugula, oil and lemon juice in medium bowl; toss gently to coat.

2 Combine ricotta, basil, ½ teaspoon salt and pepper in small bowl; mix well. Spread mixture evenly over naan; top with peach slices.

3 Bake 12 minutes or until bottom of naan is crisp. Top with arugula mixture; drizzle with vinegar and sprinkle with sea salt. Cut each flatbread into quarters.

Quick and Easy Breadsticks

makes 16 breadsticks

¼ cup (½ stick) butter, melted

¾ teaspoon garlic salt

1 container (about 14 ounces) refrigerated pizza dough

¼ cup grated Parmesan cheese

Pizza sauce or marinara sauce (optional)

1 Preheat oven to 425°F. Line baking sheet with parchment paper. Combine butter and garlic salt in small bowl; mix well.

2 Unroll dough on prepared baking sheet. Cut crosswise into 16 strips; spread strips out slightly on baking sheet close but not touching. Brush with butter mixture.

3 Bake about 8 minutes or until golden brown. Immediately sprinkle with cheese. Serve warm with pizza sauce, if desired.

Chicken Pesto Pizzas with Spinach and Tomatoes

makes 2 small pizzas

2 small (6-inch) pizza crusts

⅓ cup pesto sauce

1 cup shredded or chopped cooked chicken

1 plum tomato, thinly sliced

½ cup baby spinach, coarsely chopped

1 cup (4 ounces) shredded mozzarella cheese

1 Preheat oven to 375°F.

2 Place crusts on pizza pans or baking sheet. Spread pesto evenly over crusts; layer evenly with chicken, tomato, spinach and cheese.

3 Bake 12 to 14 minutes or until cheese is melted and crusts are golden brown.

Assorted Egg Things

Bacon and Egg Crêpes

makes 2 crêpes

2 eggs
¼ teaspoon salt
¼ teaspoon black pepper
1 teaspoon fresh thyme leaves *or* ⅛ teaspoon dried thyme
1 teaspoon butter
2 prepared crêpes
2 slices crisp-cooked bacon
2 teaspoons maple syrup

1 Whisk eggs, salt, pepper and thyme in medium bowl. Melt butter in small saucepan over medium heat. Add eggs; cook 3 to 5 minutes or until eggs are softly set, stirring and folding occasionally.

2 Divide egg mixture between crêpes. Top with bacon and drizzle with syrup. Fold up crêpes; serve immediately.

Pea and Spinach Frittata

makes 4 wedges

1 tablespoon olive oil

1 cup chopped onion

1 cup thawed frozen peas

1 cup fresh spinach

8 eggs

½ cup cooked brown rice

¼ cup milk

2 tablespoons grated Parmesan or Romano cheese, plus additional for garnish

1 tablespoon chopped fresh mint *or* 1 teaspoon dried mint

¼ teaspoon salt

¼ teaspoon black pepper

1 Heat oil in large nonstick skillet over medium-high heat. Add onion; cook and stir 5 minutes or until softened. Add peas; cook until heated through. Add spinach; cook and stir 1 minute or until spinach just begins to wilt.

2 Whisk eggs in large bowl. Stir in rice, milk, 2 tablespoons cheese, mint, salt and pepper. Pour egg mixture into skillet. Cook without stirring 2 minutes or until eggs begin to set. Run large spatula around edge of skillet, lifting edge to allow uncooked portion to flow underneath. Remove from heat when eggs are almost set but surface is still moist.

3 Cover; let stand 3 to 4 minutes or until surface is set. Sprinkle with additional cheese, if desired. Slide onto cutting board; cut into four wedges.

Bacon Gruyère Egg Bites

makes 12 egg bites

6 eggs

1 cup cottage cheese

¾ cup (3 ounces) shredded Gruyére cheese

¼ cup (1 ounce) shredded Monterey Jack cheese

¼ teaspoon white vinegar

¼ teaspoon hot pepper sauce

Salt and black pepper

6 slices bacon, cooked and crumbled

1 Preheat oven to 300°F. Generously spray 12 standard (2¼-inch) muffin cups with nonstick cooking spray.

2 Combine eggs, cottage cheese, Gruyère, Monterey Jack, vinegar, hot pepper sauce, salt and pepper in blender or food processor; blend until smooth.

3 Pour egg mixture evenly into prepared muffin cups; top with bacon (scant 1 tablespoon per cup). Press bacon lightly into egg mixture.

4 Bake 25 to 27 minutes or until set and toothpick inserted into centers comes out with a few moist crumbs. Cool in pan on wire rack 5 minutes. Loosen edges with small knife or spatula; remove to plate. Serve warm or at room temperature.

Gratin Eggs on Toast
makes 6 toasts

6 eggs
1½ tablespoons butter
1½ tablespoons all-purpose flour
1½ cups milk
2 teaspoons Dijon mustard
¼ teaspoon salt
⅛ teaspoon black pepper
½ cup (2 ounces) shredded Cheddar cheese
6 slices artisan semolina toast

1 Bring large saucepan of water to a boil. Carefully add eggs using slotted spoon. Cook 11 minutes. Drain and run under cold water or let stand in ice water until cool. Carefully peel eggs and coarsely chop.

2 Preheat broiler. Spray 13×9-inch baking pan with nonstick cooking spray; spread eggs in pan.

3 Melt butter in medium saucepan over medium-low heat. Whisk in flour; cook 1 to 2 minutes, whisking constantly. Whisk in milk; bring to a boil. Cook 1 to 2 minutes or until thickened, whisking constantly. Stir in mustard, salt and pepper.

4 Pour sauce over eggs; top with cheese. Broil 3 inches from heat source 1 to 2 minutes or until cheese is bubbly and begins to brown. Serve eggs and sauce on toast.

Kale Quiche

makes 9 squares

1 tablespoon olive oil

1 small onion, chopped

1 clove garlic, minced

3 to 4 ounces lacinato kale, cut into thin strips (about 1½ cups packed)

¾ teaspoon salt, divided

8 eggs

1 cup (4 ounces) grated Cheddar cheese

¾ cup whipping cream

¼ teaspoon black pepper

1 Preheat oven to 350°F. Spray 8-inch square baking pan with nonstick cooking spray.

2 Heat oil in medium skillet over medium-high heat. Add onion; cook and stir 3 minutes or until softened. Add garlic; cook and stir 1 minute. Add kale and ¼ teaspoon salt; cook 10 minutes, stirring occasionally. Set aside to cool slightly.

3 Beat eggs, cheese, cream, remaining ½ teaspoon salt and pepper in medium bowl until well blended. Add kale mixture; mix well. Pour into prepared pan.

4 Bake 30 to 35 minutes or until toothpick inserted into center comes out clean. Remove to wire rack; let stand 10 minutes before serving. Cut into squares.

Bacon and Egg Pizza

makes 1 pizza

1 (12-inch) prepared
  pizza crust

3 slices turkey bacon or
  regular bacon

8 eggs *or* 2 cups liquid
  egg substitute

½ cup milk

1½ tablespoons chopped
  fresh basil, divided

¼ teaspoon salt

⅛ teaspoon black
  pepper

1 tablespoon vegetable
  oil

2 plum tomatoes, thinly
  sliced

½ cup (2 ounces)
  shredded mozzarella
  cheese

¼ cup (1 ounce) shredded
  Cheddar cheese

1 Preheat oven to 450°F. Place pizza crust on 12-inch pizza pan. Bake 6 to 8 minutes or until heated through.

2 Cook bacon in large nonstick skillet over medium-high heat until crisp. Drain on paper towel-lined plate; crumble bacon when cool enough to handle.

3 Beat eggs, milk, ½ tablespoon basil, salt and pepper in medium bowl until blended. Heat oil in same skillet over medium heat. Add egg mixture; cook until mixture begins to set around edges. Gently stir eggs with spatula, allowing uncooked portions to flow underneath. Repeat stirring every 1 to 2 minutes or until eggs are just set. Remove from heat.

4 Arrange tomato slices on pizza crust; top with scrambled eggs, bacon, mozzarella cheese and Cheddar cheese. Bake 1 minute or until cheese is melted. Sprinkle with remaining 1 tablespoon basil. Cut into wedges.

Noodle Egg Nests

makes 6 nests

1 package (3 ounces) soy- or chicken-flavored ramen noodles

6 eggs

2 tablespoons milk

Salt and black pepper

Chopped fresh parsley

1 Preheat oven to 400°F. Crumble six pieces of foil into balls about half the size of standard (2½-inch) muffin cups. Spray six muffin cups and foil balls with nonstick cooking spray.

2 Fill medium saucepan half full with water; add ramen seasoning packet and bring to a boil over high heat. Add noodles; cook 1 minute to soften. Rinse and drain under cold water. Divide noodles among prepared muffin cups, pressing into bottoms and up sides. Place foil ball in each cup to help make cup shape.

3 Bake 15 minutes. Remove foil balls; bake 10 to 12 minutes or until noodles are set and lightly browned. Cool in pan 5 minutes. *Reduce oven temperature to 325°F.*

4 Carefully crack one egg into each cup. Top each egg with 1 teaspoon milk; season with salt and pepper.

5 Bake 10 to 12 minutes until egg whites are opaque and yolks are desired doneness. Top with chopped parsley. Serve warm.

Bacon and Egg Wraps

makes 4 wraps

4 eggs, beaten *or* 1 cup liquid egg substitute

¼ cup shredded Parmesan cheese

2 slices Canadian bacon, diced

½ teaspoon hot pepper sauce

¼ teaspoon black pepper

4 (7-inch) red chile tortillas or whole wheat tortillas

1 cup baby spinach

1 Preheat oven to 325°F. Spray 9-inch glass baking dish with nonstick cooking spray. Beat eggs, cheese, bacon, hot pepper sauce and black pepper in medium bowl with fork until well blended. Bake 15 minutes or until eggs are set. Remove from oven.

2 Place tortillas in oven 1 minute or until soft and pliable. Cut egg into quarters; place one wedge in center of each tortilla. Top with ¼ cup spinach. Fold bottom of tortilla to center; fold sides to center to enclose filling.

Zucchini-Tomato Frittata

makes 4 wedges

1 tablespoon olive oil

1 cup sliced zucchini

1 cup broccoli florets

1 cup diced red or yellow bell pepper

8 eggs

½ cup cottage cheese

½ cup rehydrated* sun-dried tomatoes (1 ounce dry), coarsely chopped

¼ cup chopped green onions

¼ cup chopped fresh basil

½ teaspoon salt

⅛ teaspoon ground red pepper

2 tablespoons grated Parmesan cheese

To rehydrate sun-dried tomatoes, pour 1 cup boiling water over tomatoes in small bowl. Let soak 5 to 10 minutes or until softened; drain well.

1 Preheat broiler. Heat oil in medium ovenproof skillet over medium-high heat. Add zucchini, broccoli and bell pepper; cook and stir 3 to 4 minutes or until vegetables are crisp-tender.

2 Whisk eggs, cottage cheese, tomatoes, green onions, basil, salt and ground red pepper in medium bowl until well blended. Pour egg mixture over vegetables in skillet. Cook 7 to 8 minutes or until frittata is almost firm and golden brown on bottom, gently lifting edge to allow uncooked egg to flow underneath. Remove from heat; sprinkle with cheese.

3 Broil about 5 inches from heat 3 to 5 minutes or until golden brown. Slide onto cutting board; cut into four wedges.

Smoked Salmon Omelet Roll-Ups

makes about 24 pieces

4 eggs

1/8 teaspoon black pepper

1 tablespoon vegetable oil

1/4 cup chive and onion cream cheese, softened

1 package (about 4 ounces) smoked salmon (lox), cut into bite-size pieces

1 Whisk eggs and pepper in small bowl until well blended. Heat oil in large nonstick skillet over medium-high heat.

2 Pour half of egg mixture into skillet; tilt skillet to completely coat bottom with thin layer of eggs. Cook without stirring 2 to 4 minutes or until eggs are set. Use spatula to carefully loosen omelet from skillet; slide onto cutting board. Repeat with remaining egg mixture to make second omelet.

3 Spread 2 tablespoons cream cheese over each omelet; top with smoked salmon pieces. Roll up omelets tightly; wrap in plastic wrap and refrigerate at least 30 minutes. Cut off ends, then cut rolls crosswise into 1/2-inch slices.

Spaghetti and Vegetable Frittata

makes 4 wedges

2 tablespoons butter, divided

1 package (8 ounces) sliced mushrooms

1 cup thinly sliced leeks (white and light green parts)

6 eggs

⅓ cup milk

3 tablespoons grated Parmesan cheese

¼ teaspoon salt

⅛ teaspoon ground nutmeg

⅛ teaspoon black pepper

1 package (10 ounces) frozen chopped collard greens, thawed and squeezed dry

2 cups cooked whole wheat or regular spaghetti

½ cup (2 ounces) shredded mozzarella cheese

1 Melt 1 tablespoon butter in large ovenproof skillet over medium-high heat. Add mushrooms and leeks; cook and stir 8 minutes or until lightly browned.

2 Whisk eggs, milk, Parmesan cheese, salt, nutmeg and pepper in large bowl. Stir in collard greens, spaghetti and mushroom mixture.

3 Melt remaining 1 tablespoon butter in same skillet over medium-low heat. Add egg mixture; cover and cook 10 minutes or until top is set.

4 Meanwhile, preheat broiler. Sprinkle mozzarella cheese over frittata; broil about 5 inches from heat 3 minutes or until golden brown. Slide onto cutting board; cut into four wedges.

Tip When you cook spaghetti for another dinner, make extra to save for this recipe.

Shortcut Spanish Tortilla

makes 6 wedges

2 tablespoons olive oil

1 medium onion, cut in half and thinly sliced

10 eggs

½ teaspoon salt

⅛ teaspoon black pepper

5 ounces potato chips (use plain thin chips, not kettle), lightly crushed

Chopped fresh chives or parsley (optional)

1 Preheat oven to 350°F. Spray 8-inch round cake pan with nonstick cooking spray.

2 Heat oil in medium skillet over medium-high heat. Add onion; cook and stir 5 minutes or until softened and beginning to brown. Remove from heat; set aside to cool 5 minutes.

3 Meanwhile, whisk eggs, salt and pepper in medium bowl until blended. Add potato chips; fold in gently until all chips are coated. Let stand 5 minutes to soften. Stir in onion. Pour mixture into prepared pan; smooth top.

4 Bake 25 minutes or until toothpick inserted into center comes out clean. Remove to wire rack; cool 5 minutes. Loosen tortilla from side of pan, if necessary. Invert tortilla onto plate; invert again onto large serving plate or cutting board. Sprinkle with chives, if desired. Cut into six wedges.

Pepper and Egg Pockets

makes 2 pockets

3 eggs
1 tablespoon milk
⅛ teaspoon salt
⅛ teaspoon black pepper
3 teaspoons butter, softened, divided
3 tablespoons minced red onion
2 tablespoons diced roasted red pepper
1 whole wheat pita bread, cut in half crosswise

1 Whisk eggs, milk, salt and black pepper in small bowl until well blended.

2 Melt 2 teaspoons butter in medium skillet over medium heat. Add onion; cook and stir 5 minutes or until softened. Pour egg mixture into skillet; sprinkle with roasted peppers. Stir gently, lifting edge to allow uncooked portion to flow underneath. Cook just until set.

3 Spread inside of pita halves with remaining 1 teaspoon butter. Spoon egg mixture into pita halves.

Scrambled Eggs and Tortillas

makes 2 servings

¼ cup vegetable or canola oil

2 small (6-inch) corn tortillas, cut in half and cut into ½-inch slices

¾ teaspoon salt, divided

4 eggs

1 Heat oil in medium skillet over medium-high heat until hot (tortilla strip dropped in oil will sizzle). Add tortilla strips; cook and stir 1 minute or until light golden and almost crisp. Remove with tongs to paper towel-lined plate; sprinkle with ¼ teaspoon salt. Drain all but 1 tablespoon oil.

2 Whisk eggs and remaining ½ teaspoon salt in medium bowl until well blended. Heat same skillet over medium heat. Add eggs; cook and stir about 1 minute or until almost set. Add tortilla strips; cook and stir 1 to 2 minutes or until eggs are firm.

Classic Deviled Eggs
makes 12 deviled eggs

6 eggs

3 tablespoons mayonnaise

½ teaspoon apple cider vinegar

½ teaspoon yellow mustard

⅛ teaspoon salt

Optional toppings: black pepper, paprika, minced fresh chives and/or minced red onion (optional)

1 Bring large saucepan of water to a boil. Carefully add eggs using slotted spoon. Cook 11 minutes. Drain and run under cold water or let stand in ice water until cool.

2 Carefully peel eggs. Cut eggs in half; place yolks in small bowl. Add mayonnaise, vinegar, mustard and salt; mash until well blended. Spoon mixture into egg whites; garnish with desired toppings.

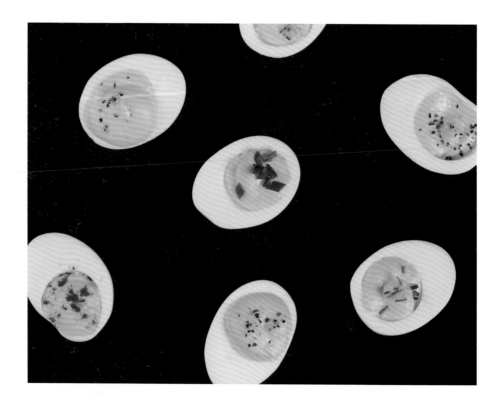

Fabulous Feta Frittata

makes 4 wedges

8 eggs

¼ cup plain Greek yogurt

¼ cup chopped fresh basil

¼ teaspoon salt

¼ teaspoon black pepper

1 tablespoon olive oil or butter

1 package (4 ounces) crumbled feta cheese with basil, olives and sun-dried tomatoes *or* 1 cup crumbled plain feta cheese

¼ cup pine nuts (optional)

1 Preheat broiler. Whisk eggs, yogurt, basil, salt and pepper in medium bowl until well blended.

2 Heat oil in large ovenproof skillet over medium heat, tilting skillet to coat bottom and side. Pour egg mixture into skillet; cover and cook 8 to 10 minutes or until eggs are set around edge (center will be wet).

3 Sprinkle feta and pine nuts, if desired, evenly over top. Transfer to broiler; broil 4 to 5 inches from heat source 2 minutes or until center is set and pine nuts are golden brown. Slide onto cutting board; cut into four wedges.

Crunchy Snacks

Choco-Peanut Butter Popcorn Chow

makes 4 cups popcorn

4 cups air-popped popcorn
⅓ cup semisweet chocolate chips
3 tablespoons peanut butter
1 tablespoon butter
½ cup powdered sugar

1 Place popcorn in large bowl. Heat chocolate chips, peanut butter and butter in medium microwavable bowl on HIGH 30 seconds; stir. Microwave 30 seconds or until melted and smooth. Pour mixture over popcorn; stir until evenly coated.

2 Place powdered sugar in 1-gallon resealable food storage bag. Add popcorn. Seal bag; shake until well coated. Spread onto waxed paper to cool. Store leftovers in airtight container in refrigerator.

Parmesan Ranch Snack Mix

makes 9½ cups snack mix

3 cups corn or rice cereal squares

2 cups oyster crackers

1 package (5 ounces) bagel chips, broken in half

1½ cups mini pretzel twists

1 cup shelled pistachio nuts

2 tablespoons grated Parmesan cheese

¼ cup (½ stick) butter, melted

1 package (1 ounce) dry ranch salad dressing mix

½ teaspoon garlic powder

Slow Cooker Directions

1 Combine cereal, oyster crackers, bagel chips, pretzels, pistachios and cheese in slow cooker.

2 Combine butter, salad dressing mix and garlic powder in small bowl. Pour over cereal mixture; toss lightly to coat. Cover; cook on LOW 3 hours.

3 Remove cover; stir gently. Cook, uncovered, on LOW 30 minutes. Store leftovers in airtight container.

Maple-Cinnamon Almonds

makes about 3½ cups nuts

¼ cup maple-flavored syrup

3 tablespoons butter

2 tablespoons sugar

1½ teaspoons ground cinnamon

¼ teaspoon salt

1 pound blanched whole almonds

¼ cup coarse white decorating sugar (optional)

1 Preheat oven to 325°F. Line two 15×10-inch sheet pans with foil.

2 Combine syrup, butter, sugar, cinnamon and salt in heavy medium saucepan. Bring to a boil over high heat, stirring frequently; boil 30 seconds. Remove from heat; stir in almonds with wooden spoon until evenly coated. Spread almond mixture in single layer in one prepared pan.

3 Bake about 40 minutes or until almonds are crisp and dry, stirring every 15 minutes. Immediately transfer almonds to remaining prepared pan; sprinkle evenly with coarse sugar. Cool completely. Store in airtight container at room temperature up to 1 week.

Sweet Ramen Nuggets

makes about 8 cups nuggets

4 packages (3 ounces each) ramen noodles*

1 cup semisweet chocolate chips

1 cup butterscotch chips

¾ cup creamy peanut butter

¼ cup (½ stick) butter

1½ cups powdered sugar

Use any flavor; discard seasoning packets.

1 Break noodles into bite-size pieces; place in large bowl.

2 Combine chocolate chips, butterscotch chips, peanut butter and butter in large microwavable bowl. Microwave on HIGH 1 minute; stir. Continue to microwave at 30-second intervals, stirring until smooth.

3 Pour chocolate mixture over noodles; stir to coat evenly.

4 Line large baking sheet with parchment or waxed paper. Place powdered sugar in 1-gallon resealable food storage bag; add noodle mixture. Seal bag; shake until well coated. Spread in single layer on prepared baking sheet; let stand until set. Store in airtight container.

Hot Buttery Mixed Nuts

makes about 3 cups

¼ cup (½ stick) butter

2 cloves garlic, crushed

1 cup pecan halves

1 cup shelled pistachio nuts

1 cup whole cashew nuts

½ cup whole almonds

½ to ⅔ cup lightly crushed canned onion rings

1 to 1¼ teaspoons chipotle chile powder*

½ teaspoon salt

½ teaspoon ground cumin

½ teaspoon smoked paprika

For milder flavor, use ¾ to 1 teaspoon; for more spiciness, use 1¼ teaspoons.

1 Preheat oven to 300°F. Melt butter in large heavy saucepan over low heat. Stir in garlic; remove from heat. Cover and let stand 5 minutes.

2 Remove garlic with slotted spoon. Add pecans, pistachios, cashews, almonds, onion rings, chili powder, salt, cumin and paprika; stir gently to coat nuts with butter and spices. Spread evenly on ungreased rimmed baking sheet.

3 Bake 16 to 20 minutes or until nuts are fragrant and golden brown, stirring after 10 minutes. Cool completely on baking sheet. Store in airtight container.

Basic Board

makes 1 board

2 to 3 kinds of cheese (one soft like Brie, one firm like aged Cheddar or Gouda)

1 to 2 kinds of meat (smoked sausage, pepperoni, prosciutto)

1 to 2 fruits (grapes, apples, pears, dried apricots, fresh or dried cherries)

1 to 2 kinds of nuts (smoked or roasted almonds, mixed nuts, candied pecans)

Assorted crackers and toasts

Dips and spreads like honey, mustard, butter or pesto sauce

1 Arrange cheeses, meats, fruits, nuts and crackers on cutting board or plate.

2 Place dips in small bowls and place on board.

Tip Make your board as fancy (or not) as you want. The cheese section of the grocery store has all manner of crackers, spreads and nuts that go well with cheese. Try marcona almonds, fig jam, red pepper jelly, hot honey, cornichons and anything else that looks interesting. To make your board extra fancy, try a recipe or two. Hot Buttery Mixed Nuts (page 156), Apricot and Brie Dip (page 10) or Citrus Candied Nuts (page 162) are all amazing on a board.

Cinnamon Toast Poppers

makes 6 cups poppers

6 cups fresh bread* cubes (1-inch cubes)

2 tablespoons butter, melted

2 tablespoons sugar

½ teaspoon ground cinnamon

Use a firm sourdough, whole wheat or semolina bread.

1 Preheat oven to 325°F. Place bread cubes in large bowl. Drizzle with butter; toss to coat.

2 Combine sugar and cinnamon in small bowl. Sprinkle over bread; mix well.

3 Spread bread cubes in single layer on ungreased baking sheet. Bake 25 minutes or until bread is golden and fragrant, stirring once or twice. Serve warm or at room temperature.

Party Popcorn

makes 6 quarts

¼ cup vegetable oil

½ cup unpopped popcorn kernels

1 teaspoon fine sea salt or popcorn salt

4 ounces almond bark,* chopped

Rainbow nonpareils

Look for almond bark by the chocolate chips in the baking aisle of the grocery store. It is a confectionery coating and does not actually contain almonds.

1 Line two baking sheets with parchment paper.

2 Heat oil in large saucepan over medium-high heat 1 minute. Add popcorn; cover with lid and cook 2 to 3 minutes or until popcorn slows to about 1 second between pops, carefully shaking pan occasionally.

3 Spread popcorn on prepared baking sheets; immediately sprinkle with salt and toss gently to blend.

4 Melt almond bark according to package directions. Drizzle over popcorn; sprinkle with nonpareils. Let stand until set.

Citrus Candied Nuts

makes 3 cups nuts

1 egg white
¼ teaspoon salt
1½ cups whole almonds
1½ cups pecan halves
1 cup powdered sugar
2 tablespoons lemon juice
2 teaspoons grated orange peel
1 teaspoon grated lemon peel
⅛ teaspoon ground nutmeg

1 Preheat oven to 300°F. Lightly grease large baking sheet.

2 Beat egg white and salt in medium bowl with electric mixer at high speed until soft peaks form. Add almonds and pecans; stir until well coated. Stir in powdered sugar, lemon juice, orange peel, lemon peel and nutmeg until evenly coated. Spread nuts in single layer on prepared baking sheet.

3 Bake 30 minutes, stirring after 20 minutes. Turn off heat. Let nuts stand in oven 15 minutes. Spread nuts on large sheet of foil; cool completely. Store in airtight container.

Chili Cashews

makes 2 cups nuts

1 tablespoon vegetable oil

2 teaspoons chili powder

1 teaspoon ground cumin

½ teaspoon sugar

½ teaspoon red pepper flakes

2 cups roasted salted whole cashews (about 9 ounces)

1 Preheat oven to 350°F. Line baking sheet with foil; spray with nonstick cooking spray.

2 Combine oil, chili powder, cumin, sugar and red pepper flakes in medium bowl; stir until well blended. Add cashews, stirring to coat evenly. Spread in single layer on prepared baking sheet.

3 Bake 8 to 10 minutes or until golden, stirring once. Cool completely on baking sheet.

Sweets for Supper

Double Pineapple Berry Dump Cake

makes 12 to 16 servings

1 can (20 ounces) crushed pineapple, undrained

1 package (12 ounces) frozen mixed berries, thawed and drained

1 package (about 15 ounces) pineapple cake mix

½ cup (1 stick) butter, cut into thin slices

Whipped cream or vanilla ice cream (optional)

1 Preheat oven to 350°F. Spray 13×9-inch baking pan with nonstick cooking spray.

2 Spread pineapple and berries in prepared pan. Top with cake mix, spreading evenly. Top with butter in single layer, covering cake mix as much as possible.

3 Bake 45 to 50 minutes or until toothpick inserted into center of cake comes out clean. Cool at least 15 minutes before serving. Serve with whipped cream, if desired.

Lemon-Raspberry Cake

makes 1 serving

3 tablespoons all-purpose flour

2 tablespoons granulated sugar

¼ teaspoon baking powder

Pinch of salt

2 tablespoons milk

1 tablespoon sour cream

1 tablespoon plus 1 teaspoon lemon juice, divided

½ tablespoon vegetable oil

¼ cup fresh raspberries

2 tablespoons powdered sugar

1 Combine flour, granulated sugar, baking powder and salt in large microwavable mug; mix well. Add milk, sour cream, milk, 1 tablespoon lemon juice and oil; stir until well blended. Top with raspberries.

2 Microwave on HIGH 2 minutes. Let stand 10 minutes before serving.

3 Combine powdered sugar and remaining 1 teaspoon lemon juice in small bowl; stir until smooth. Drizzle glaze over cake. Serve immediately.

Variation You can also use fresh blueberries, strawberries or blackberries or a combination.

Fudgy Marshmallow Popcorn

makes about 4 quarts

3½ quarts popped popcorn (about 14 cups)

2 cups sugar

1 cup evaporated milk

¼ cup (½ stick) butter

1 cup marshmallow creme (½ of 7-ounce jar)

1 cup semisweet chocolate chips

1 teaspoon vanilla

1 Spray baking sheets with nonstick cooking spray or line with parchment paper. Place popcorn in large bowl.

2 Combine sugar, evaporated milk and butter in medium saucepan. Cook over medium heat until sugar is dissolved and mixture comes to a boil, stirring constantly.* Boil 5 minutes. Remove from heat. Stir in marshmallow creme, chocolate chips and vanilla until chocolate is melted and mixture is smooth.

3 Pour chocolate mixture over popcorn, stirring until completely coated. Spread in single layer on prepared baking sheets. Refrigerate until set.

*If sugar mixture sticks to the pan, wash down side of pan with pastry brush dipped in hot water to remove crystals.

Hint Remove any unpopped kernels before measuring the popped popcorn.

Cookie Dough Monkey Bread

makes about 16 servings

1 package (about 16 ounces) break-apart refrigerated chocolate chip cookie dough (24 cookies)

2 packages (7½ ounces each) refrigerated buttermilk biscuits (10 biscuits per package)

1 cup semisweet chocolate chips, divided

¼ cup whipping cream

1 Preheat oven to 350°F. Generously spray 12-cup (10-inch) bundt pan with nonstick cooking spray.

2 Break cookie dough into 24 pieces; split each piece in half to create 48 pieces. Separate biscuits; cut each biscuit into four pieces with scissors. Layer half of cookie dough and half of biscuit pieces in prepared pan, alternating doughs. Sprinkle with ¼ cup chocolate chips. Repeat layers of cookie dough and biscuit pieces; sprinkle with ¼ cup chocolate chips.

3 Bake 27 to 30 minutes or until biscuits are golden brown, covering pan loosely with foil during last 10 minutes of baking. Remove pan to wire rack; let stand, covered, 5 minutes. Loosen edges of bread with knife; invert onto serving plate.

4 Place remaining ½ cup chocolate chips in small bowl. Bring cream to a simmer in small saucepan over medium-heat. Pour over chips; stir until chocolate is melted. Let stand 5 minutes to thicken slightly. Drizzle glaze over bread.

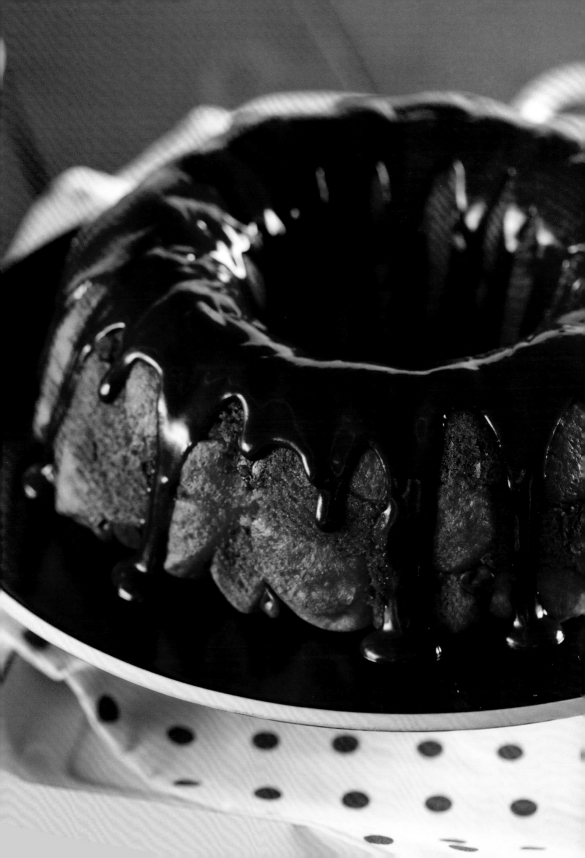

Peppermint Chip Cake in a Cup

makes 1 serving

¼ cup angel food cake mix

3 tablespoons water

1 tablespoon mini semisweet chocolate chips, plus additional for garnish

2 tablespoons thawed frozen whipped topping

⅛ teaspoon peppermint extract

Crushed peppermints* (optional)

*To crush peppermints, place unwrapped candy in a heavy-duty resealable food storage bag. Loosely seal the bag, leaving an opening for air to escape. Crush the candies thoroughly with a rolling pin, meat mallet or the bottom of a heavy skillet.

1 Combine cake mix, water and 1 tablespoon chocolate chips in large ceramic** microwavable mug.

2 Microwave on HIGH 1½ minutes. Let stand 1 to 2 minutes.

3 Meanwhile, stir whipped topping and peppermint extract in small bowl until well blended. Spoon over cake. Top with additional chocolate chips and crushed peppermints, if desired. Serve immediately.

**This cake will only work in a ceramic mug as the material allows for more even cooking than glass.

Cinnamon-Sugar Waffles

makes 6 waffles

¾ cup sugar

2 teaspoons ground cinnamon

1½ teaspoons ground nutmeg

1¼ cups all-purpose flour

½ cup whole wheat flour

2 teaspoons baking powder

½ teaspoon salt

1¾ cups buttermilk

2 eggs

6 tablespoons butter, melted and cooled slightly

1½ teaspoons vanilla

1 Preheat Belgian or classic waffle maker to medium-high heat.

2 Combine sugar, cinnamon and nutmeg in small bowl. Place ½ cup sugar mixture in large bowl; pour remaining mixture into large resealable food storage bag.

3 Add flours, baking powder and salt to ½ cup sugar mixture in large bowl. Combine buttermilk, eggs, butter and vanilla in small bowl; stir into dry ingredients just until blended.

4 Place scant ¾ cup batter in center of waffle maker. Close lid and cook 3 to 5 minutes or until waffle is golden brown. Place hot waffle in sugar mixture in bag; seal bag and shake until evenly coated. Remove to wire rack. Repeat with remaining batter.

Tip For an extra special entrée, sandwich vanilla ice cream between two waffles.

Pound Cake Dip Sticks

makes 8 to 10 servings

½ cup raspberry jam, divided

1 package (about 10 ounces) frozen pound cake, thawed

1½ cups cold whipping cream

1 Preheat oven to 400°F. Spray baking sheet with nonstick cooking spray. Microwave ¼ cup jam in small bowl on HIGH 30 seconds or until smooth.

2 Cut pound cake into 10 (½-inch) slices. Brush one side of slices lightly with warm jam. Cut each slice lengthwise into three sticks. Place sticks, jam side up, on prepared baking sheet.

3 Bake 10 minutes or until cake sticks are crisp and light golden brown. Remove to wire rack.

4 Meanwhile, beat cream in large bowl with electric mixer until soft peaks form. Add remaining ¼ cup raspberry jam; beat until combined. Serve with cake sticks.

Chocolate-Almond Crispy Treats

makes 24 bars

6 cups crisp brown rice cereal

1½ cups sliced almonds, toasted*

1 cup light corn syrup

⅓ cup almond butter

¼ cup packed brown sugar

3 tablespoons unsweetened cocoa powder

¼ teaspoon salt

1 cup semisweet chocolate chips

To toast almonds, spread in single layer in heavy skillet. Cook over medium heat 1 to 2 minutes or until nuts are lightly browned, stirring frequently.

1 Line 13×9-inch baking pan with parchment paper. Spray with nonstick cooking spray.

2 Combine rice cereal and almonds in large bowl.

3 Combine corn syrup, almond butter, brown sugar, cocoa and salt in large saucepan. Cook and stir over medium heat 5 minutes or until mixture is smooth and just begins to boil across surface. Remove from heat.

4 Immediately stir cereal mixture into saucepan. Gently fold in chocolate chips. Press firmly into prepared pan. Let stand 1 hour or until set. Cut into bars.

Chocolate and Peanut Butter Molten Cake

makes 1 serving

¼ cup all-purpose flour

1 tablespoon unsweetened cocoa powder

2½ tablespoons sugar

¼ teaspoon baking powder

Pinch of salt

¼ cup milk

2 tablespoons butter, melted

¼ teaspoon vanilla

1 teaspoon peanut butter

2 teaspoons mini semisweet chocolate chips, divided

1 Combine flour, cocoa, sugar, baking powder and salt in medium bowl; mix well. Add milk, butter and vanilla; stir until well blended. Pour batter into large microwavable mug or ramekin.

2 Place peanut butter and 1 teaspoon chocolate chips in center of batter; press down slightly.

3 Microwave on HIGH 1 minute. Let stand 10 minutes before serving. Sprinkle with remaining 1 teaspoon chocolate chips.

Cracker Toffee

makes about 24 pieces

72 rectangular butter-flavored crackers
1 cup (2 sticks) butter
1 cup packed brown sugar
¼ teaspoon salt
2½ cups semisweet chocolate chips
2 cups chopped pecans

1 Preheat oven to 375°F. Line 17×12-inch baking pan with foil. Spray generously with nonstick cooking spray. Arrange crackers with edges touching in pan.

2 Combine butter, brown sugar and salt in heavy medium saucepan. Heat over medium heat until butter melts, stirring frequently. Increase heat to high; boil 3 minutes without stirring. Pour mixture evenly over crackers; spread to cover.

3 Bake 5 minutes. Immediately sprinkle chocolate chips evenly over crackers; spread to cover. Sprinkle pecans over chocolate, pressing down. Cool to room temperature. Refrigerate 2 hours. Break into chunks to serve.

Variation Substitute peanut butter chips for chocolate chips and coarsely chopped peanuts for chopped pecans.

Apple Pie Monkey Bread

makes 8 servings

½ cup (1 stick) butter, divided

2 large apples (about 1 pound), peeled and cut into ½-inch pieces (Fuji, Granny Smith or Braeburn)

½ cup plus 1 tablespoon sugar, divided

2½ teaspoons ground cinnamon, divided

½ cup finely chopped pecans

1 package (12 ounces) refrigerated buttermilk biscuits (10 biscuits per package)

1 Preheat oven to 350°F. Spray 9-inch pie plate with nonstick cooking spray.

2 Melt ¼ cup butter in large skillet or saucepan over medium heat. Add apples, 1 tablespoon sugar and ½ teaspoon cinnamon; cook and stir 5 minutes or until apples are tender and glazed. Transfer to large bowl. Melt remaining ¼ cup butter in same skillet, stirring to scrape up any glaze. Cool slightly.

3 Combine pecans, remaining ½ cup sugar and 2 teaspoons cinnamon in medium bowl. Separate biscuits; cut each biscuit into six pieces with scissors. Dip biscuit pieces in melted butter; roll in pecan mixture to coat. Place one fourth of biscuit pieces in prepared pie plate; top with one fourth of apples. Repeat layers three times. Sprinkle with remaining pecan mixture and drizzle with any remaining butter.

4 Bake about 28 minutes or until biscuits are firm and topping is golden brown. Serve warm.

Tropical Dump Cake

makes 12 to 16 servings

1 can (20 ounces) crushed pineapple, undrained

1 can (15 ounces) peach slices in light syrup, undrained

1 package (about 15 ounces) yellow cake mix

½ cup (1 stick) butter, cut into thin slices

1 cup packed brown sugar

½ cup flaked coconut

½ cup chopped pecans

1 Preheat oven to 350°F. Spray 13×9-inch baking pan with nonstick cooking spray.

2 Spread pineapple and peaches in prepared pan. Top with cake mix, spreading evenly. Top with butter in single layer, covering cake mix as much as possible. Sprinkle with brown sugar, coconut and pecans.

3 Bake 40 to 45 minutes or until toothpick inserted into center of cake comes out clean. Cool at least 15 minutes before serving.

Doughnut Hole Fondue

makes 6 servings

¾ cup whipping cream
1 cup bittersweet or semisweet chocolate chips
1 tablespoon butter
½ teaspoon vanilla
12 to 16 doughnut holes
Sliced fresh fruit, such as pineapple, bananas, strawberries, melon and oranges

1 Heat cream in small saucepan until bubbles form around edge. Remove from heat. Add chocolate; let stand 2 minutes or until softened. Add butter and vanilla; whisk until smooth. Keep warm in fondue pot or transfer to serving bowl.

2 Serve with doughnut holes and fruit.

¶Index

Index

Metric Conversion Chart

VOLUME MEASUREMENTS (dry)

¹/₈ teaspoon = 0.5 mL
¹/₄ teaspoon = 1 mL
¹/₂ teaspoon = 2 mL
³/₄ teaspoon = 4 mL
1 teaspoon = 5 mL
1 tablespoon = 15 mL
2 tablespoons = 30 mL
¹/₄ cup = 60 mL
¹/₃ cup = 75 mL
¹/₂ cup = 125 mL
²/₃ cup = 150 mL
³/₄ cup = 175 mL
1 cup = 250 mL
2 cups = 1 pint = 500 mL
3 cups = 750 mL
4 cups = 1 quart = 1 L

VOLUME MEASUREMENTS (fluid)

1 fluid ounce (2 tablespoons) = 30 mL
4 fluid ounces (¹/₂ cup) = 125 mL
8 fluid ounces (1 cup) = 250 mL
12 fluid ounces (1¹/₂ cups) = 375 mL
16 fluid ounces (2 cups) = 500 mL

WEIGHTS (mass)

¹/₂ ounce = 15 g
1 ounce = 30 g
3 ounces = 90 g
4 ounces = 120 g
8 ounces = 225 g
10 ounces = 285 g
12 ounces = 360 g
16 ounces = 1 pound = 450 g

DIMENSIONS

¹/₁₆ inch = 2 mm
¹/₈ inch = 3 mm
¹/₄ inch = 6 mm
¹/₂ inch = 1.5 cm
³/₄ inch = 2 cm
1 inch = 2.5 cm

OVEN TEMPERATURES

250°F = 120°C
275°F = 140°C
300°F = 150°C
325°F = 160°C
350°F = 180°C
375°F = 190°C
400°F = 200°C
425°F = 220°C
450°F = 230°C

BAKING PAN SIZES

Utensil	Size in Inches/Quarts	Metric Volume	Size in Centimeters
Baking or Cake Pan (square or rectangular)	8×8×2	2 L	20×20×5
	9×9×2	2.5 L	23×23×5
	12×8×2	3 L	30×20×5
	13×9×2	3.5 L	33×23×5
Loaf Pan	8×4×3	1.5 L	20×10×7
	9×5×3	2 L	23×13×7
Round Layer Cake Pan	8×1½	1.2 L	20×4
	9×1½	1.5 L	23×4
Pie Plate	8×1¼	750 mL	20×3
	9×1¼	1 L	23×3
Baking Dish or Casserole	1 quart	1 L	—
	1½ quart	1.5 L	—
	2 quart	2 L	—